Mindfulness

The Science and Practice of Well-being

Jane Frey

Stone Arrow

Contents

Introduction

DEFINITION AND ORIGINS

Mindfulness can radically change your life for the better.

Mindfulness is a mental state where you're aware of the present moment. Mindfulness practice involves paying attention to one's thoughts, emotions, and sensations in a non-judgmental and accepting way. This can include observing the breath, noticing physical sensations in the body, and paying attention to thoughts and emotions as they arise.

The goal of mindfulness is not to suppress or control thoughts and emotions but to develop a greater awareness of them and cultivate a sense of calm and clarity.

Mindfulness has been a central component in Eastern philosophy and religions such as Buddhism and Hinduism for thousands of years. Followers of these traditions use mindfulness to cultivate inner peace and wisdom.

In recent decades, mindfulness has been adapted and applied in a secular context, and it is now widely used to improve mental and physical health.

Studies show that mindfulness has many benefits, including reduced stress and improved mental and physical health. It has been used in various settings, such as schools, hospitals, and the workplace, to promote well-being and improve individuals' and groups' mental and physical health.

Mindfulness practice involves paying attention to the present moment in a non-judgmental and accepting way. This can include observing the breath, noticing physical sensations in the body, and paying attention to thoughts and emotions as they arise. The goal of mindfulness is not to suppress or control thoughts and emotions but to develop a greater awareness of them and to cultivate a sense of calm and clarity.

You can incorporate mindfulness into daily activities and routines, such as eating, exercising, and commuting. You can also practice it in a dedicated mindfulness session, such as a formal meditation practice. In either case, your goal is to bring a sense of mindfulness to the present moment and to cultivate a greater awareness of your thoughts, emotions, and sensations.

In this book, we will explore the science behind mindfulness and its potential benefits, as well as the latest research on its effectiveness and practical tips for using mindfulness in daily life.

Chapter Two

Origins

Mindfulness, meditation and you

Mindfulness has its roots in ancient Eastern spiritual traditions, such as Buddhism and Hinduism. The concept of mindfulness has been central to these traditions for thousands of years and has been adapted and incorporated into various spiritual and philosophical practices.

In the Buddhist tradition, mindfulness is seen as one of the seven factors of enlightenment and is closely related to meditation. The Buddha himself emphasized the importance of mindfulness in his teachings. Many core principles of Buddhist philosophy, such as the Four Noble Truths and the Eightfold Path, can be understood as ways of cultivating mindfulness.

In Hinduism, mindfulness is a critical component of the spiritual discipline of yoga. The goal of yoga is to cultivate inner peace and clarity, and mindfulness is seen as a crucial tool in achieving this. The ancient text of the Bhagavad Gita, one of the most sacred texts in Hinduism, emphasizes the importance of mindfulness in pursuing spiritual growth and enlightenment.

The relationship between mindfulness and meditation is complex and multi-faceted. Meditation is often seen as a way of practising mindfulness, and many mindfulness techniques are based on meditative practices. For example, mindful breathing, in which one focuses on the breath and lets go of distracting thoughts, is a form of meditation commonly used in mindfulness training.

However, you can also practice mindfulness outside formal meditation in everyday activities such as eating, walking, and interacting with others. In this way, mindfulness is a meditative practice and a way of being present and aware in all aspects of life.

CHAPTER THREE

Misconceptions

COMMON MISUNDERSTANDINGS AND MYTHS

Probably the most significant misconception people have about mindfulness is that it's confused with meditation.

Some people use mindfulness and meditation interchangeably, but it is essential to recognize that they are not the same thing. You can practice mindfulness in many ways, and meditation is just one of them.

Meditation is a specific practice involving focusing the mind on a single point of attention, such as the breath or a mantra, to cultivate mental clarity and stillness. Through the practice of meditation, you can learn to quiet the mind and develop the ability to focus your attention on the present moment.

While meditation is a powerful tool for cultivating mindfulness, it is not the only way to do so. You can practice mindfulness in many different ways and do not need to meditate to experience mindfulness.

For example, you can practice mindfulness while walking, eating, or doing any other activity that allows you to pay attention to the present moment without distraction. These practices can help to quiet the mind and bring your attention to the present moment, allowing you to experience mindfulness.

Mindfulness is a broader concept that refers to being present and aware in the moment, without judgment or attachment. It is a mental state of being aware of and present in the moment. It involves paying attention to your thoughts, feelings, and surroundings without judging or reacting. This state of mind can be beneficial because it allows you to experience the present moment entirely and without distraction.

Some other misconceptions commonly occur – let's look at each quickly and clear up any misunderstandings.

Mindfulness is Buddhism

This is a common misconception, but mindfulness is not inherently tied to Buddhism or any other religion. While Buddhists often use mindfulness as a part of Buddhist meditation, it can be practised by people of any faith or belief, or by those who do not follow any specific religion.

Mindfulness requires a lot of time

Another common misconception is that mindfulness requires a lot of time to practice. While it is true that some mindfulness exercises, such as formal meditation, can take longer, you can incorporate mindfulness into everyday activities, even for a few minutes at a time.

Mindfulness is about being boring, calm, and complacent

Some may think mindfulness means being free of all thoughts and emotions, but this is not the case. Mindfulness involves allowing thoughts and feelings to arise and pass without judgment or attachment rather than trying to eliminate them. Mindfulness can lead to greater vitality and engagement in life rather than complacency.

Mindfulness 'fixes' you

Mindfulness is not a quick fix or a cure-all for mental health issues, but it can be a helpful tool for managing stress, anxiety, and other mental health concerns. Mindfulness can help to improve overall well-being and to reduce negative thought patterns, but it is not a replacement for medical treatment or therapy.

Mindfulness is a form of brainwashing

This is a false and misleading idea. Mindfulness is a mental state that involves being aware of one's thoughts, feelings, and surroundings, and it does not include any form of manipulation or control.

Mindfulness is only for adults

While mindfulness can be particularly beneficial for adults, it can also be helpful for children and teenagers. Mindfulness can help children develop greater focus and attention, improving their overall well-being. There is no age limit to practising mindfulness; anyone can benefit from it.

Mindfulness is for those who are already calm

Mindfulness can help to reduce negative thought patterns and improve overall mental well-being. Some may think mindfulness is only relevant for people who are already calm and relaxed. In reality, mindfulness benefits people who struggle with anxiety, stress, or other mental health issues.

Mindfulness is only for calm and quiet settings

While you can practice mindfulness in a calm and quiet setting, you can also incorporate it into everyday activities. You'll find it will help you manage stress and improve focus and attention in any situation.

Mindfulness is just a trendy fad

Mindfulness has been practised for thousands of years and is not a passing trend or fad. While mindfulness has recently gained popularity, it is a well-established and effective tool for improving mental and emotional well-being.

CHAPTER FOUR

Science of Mindfulness

RESEARCH FINDINGS AND BENEFITS

In recent years, mindfulness has gained widespread recognition as a powerful tool for promoting mental and physical health. But what does the science say about the benefits of mindfulness? In this chapter, we will review the research on the effectiveness of mindfulness in reducing symptoms of stress and anxiety, improving focus and concentration, and promoting overall well-being. We will also discuss some of the mechanisms behind these benefits.

Two Types of Mindfulness Training

Mindfulness-based cognitive therapy (MBCT) and mindfulness-based stress reduction (MBSR) are two different types of mindfulness training programs. Both of these programs are based on the principles of mindfulness. However, there are some critical differences between MBCT and MBSR.

MBCT is a form of therapy used to prevent relapse in people with a history of depression. It combines the principles of cognitive therapy, which focuses on changing negative thought patterns, with mindfulness practices. MBCT aims to help people learn to recognize and respond to negative thoughts and emotions more positively and constructively.

MBSR, on the other hand, is a program designed to help people reduce stress and improve their overall well-being. MBSR aims to help people develop greater resilience and coping skills in response to stress. It involves a series of mindfulness practices, such as body awareness, mindful breathing, and mindful movement, designed to help people become more aware of their thoughts and emotions.

One key difference between MBCT and MBSR is their focus. MBCT is specifically designed to help people with a history of depression, while MBSR is designed to help people reduce stress and improve their overall well-being. Additionally, MBCT focuses more on changing negative thought patterns, while MBSR focuses more on mindfulness practices and developing coping skills.

Overall, MBCT and MBSR are both effective mindfulness training programs that can help people improve their mental health and well-being. However, they differ in their focus and the length of the program.

In this book, we lean towards the techniques of MBSR – MBCT is often done with a trained professional.

What Happens When We Practice?

When we practice mindful meditation, we create a unique state of activation in the brain. This state can become an enduring trait, leading to long-term changes in the structure and function of the brain. This is because the brain can change in response to experience. Meditation aims to focus our attention on a particular aspect of the experience.

The exact components of MBSR that can make it effective are not known. However, the experience of listening to poetry, engaging in yoga, and reflecting on life's stresses can contribute to the program's scientific effectiveness.

One of the most critical factors that can contribute to the program's success is the practice of mindful meditation. In one study, participants who practised this type of meditation saw a four-fold increase in their healing rate for psoriasis. In other studies, the effects of the practice were maintained for a long time.

Physical Benefits

Incorporating mindfulness into your daily routine can positively affect your physical well-being. Here is what we know so far.

It changes your brain structure

It's believed that mindfulness can help prevent cognitive decline. A study revealed that the brains of people who practice mindfulness are more protected against losing gray matter (fewer brain cells lost!).

In 2017, a study on healthy older adults revealed that meditation could improve brain function.

It can improve your immune system

A study on eight participants revealed that those who practised mindfulness for eight weeks had more flu antibodies (and positive feelings) than those who didn't.

A study at the University of California revealed that mindfulness could improve the immune function of individuals with HIV.

It can help your heart

It's believed that mindfulness can help lower blood pressure and reduce the risk of heart disease. In a study, people with pre-diabetes were randomly assigned to either a course about mindful meditation or a program emphasising progressive muscle relaxation. The results showed that those who participated in the meditation program had lower blood pressure than those who did not.

In another study, participants with heart disease who were taking part in regular treatment for their condition were randomly assigned to either a wait-list for the meditation program or an online program that taught them how to practice mindfulness. The results showed that those in the mindfulness group experienced significant improvements in their walking test scores and heart rate.

It's believed that being mindful can help improve the health of people who are already relatively healthy. According to researchers, regular meditation can trigger respiratory arrhythmia, leading to better heart health. It can also increase the chance of surviving a heart attack.

It can slow your ageing

The natural process of cell ageing involves the repeated division of cells over a lifespan. It can be triggered by stress or disease, and the end of chromosomes refers to the protein that helps protect cells from ageing. According to studies, mindfulness meditation can affect the length of telomeres (protective structures at the ends of chromosomes that shorten as we age, which healthy lifestyle habits can slow down).

In a study, researchers discovered that breast cancer survivors who took part in MBSR had longer telomeres than those on a waitlist.

A second study with breast cancer survivors revealed that the participants had similar telomeres, although they experienced different activity levels related to cell ageing. In 2018, a research review revealed that mindfulness training could indirectly affect the integrity of telomeres in our cells.

A third study concluded that loving-kindness meditation could help slow down biological ageing. It's believed that this finding could be why scientists are more optimistic about the potential of meditation to prevent ageing.

It can help your sleep

In a study, 54 adults with chronic insomnia were taught a mindfulness-based stress reduction program. They then enrolled in either a self-monitoring program or a meditation-based program. The results of the study revealed that both programs helped improve sleep.

It can help ease pain

A 2020 a report stated that stress reduction could help improve the quality of life for people with low-back pain.

A review of 30 studies conducted in 2017 revealed that mindfulness meditation can reduce chronic pain. However, the studies that were examined were not of high quality, and further studies need to be done.

Mental Benefits

It helps with anxiety and depression

Two studies, published in 2000 and 2008, showed that mindfulness significantly reduced the relapse rate among patients who suffered from depression. A study published in The Lancet revealed that combining the program with medication can be as effective as maintaining the same dosage.

According to a meta-analysis, meditation can help people with stress-related conditions such as depression and anxiety. It found that regular meditation can reduce the harmful effects of psychological stress. The effects of this type of therapy are comparable to those of antidepressant medications.

A review of nine clinical trials revealed that MBCT can reduce the likelihood of patients returning to the depressive state for up to 60 weeks.

It can improve mental clarity

A meta-analysis of 18 studies conducted on the effects of mindfulness-based stress reduction and cognitive therapy revealed that these programs can support various cognitive components. These include short-term memory, autobiographical memory, and meta-awareness, skills that help individuals develop new ways of thinking.

Numerous studies revealed that training participants in mindfulness meditation can improve their attentional regulation. These studies also showed that the participants were more focused on the present stimulus when compared to the previous one.

It can improve mental health treatment

According to researchers, adding mindfulness-based practices to a patient's treatment is often beneficial in treating various mental health conditions, such as drug addiction and obsessive-compulsive disorder. It can also help prevent people from developing chronic depression.

Another study looked to gain a deeper understanding of the various mechanisms underlying mental disorders' treatment. After eight weeks of mindfulness-based practice, the subjects improved their brain function.

Developing a deeper understanding of ourselves could help people avoid developing destructive and repetitive thoughts. It could also help them identify their own unique streams of awareness.

It can improve your self-confidence

Although meditation can help people improve their skills as a role model, it does not enhance their abilities to enable others to act, according to the author of a study.

A group of researchers conducted a survey to measure the self-perception of senior managers in London. They then trained them through a 12-week course of meditation. Their results showed that the training significantly improved the managers' skills and confidence.

It can reduce stress

One of the mechanisms by which mindfulness may help reduce stress and anxiety is by promoting the regulation of emotions. Emotion regulation is managing and responding to emotions in a healthy and adaptive way. Mindfulness has been shown to increase awareness of emotions and help individuals develop healthier ways of responding to them. In a study, mindfulness training was associated with increased emotional awareness and reduced emotional reactivity, leading to improved emotional well-being.

One of the key findings of research on mindfulness is that it can help reduce stress and anxiety. Stress and anxiety are common mental health problems that can have a negative impact on physical health, relationships, and overall well-being. Mindfulness-based interventions, such as mindfulness-based stress reduction (MBSR) and mindfulness-based cognitive therapy (MBCT), are effective in reducing stress and anxiety symptoms in a variety of populations.

In a study, participants who received mindfulness-based therapy reported significant reductions in stress and anxiety symptoms compared to those in the control group. These reductions were maintained at follow-up assessments, indicating that the benefits of mindfulness are long-lasting. Another study found that mindfulness training was effective in reducing anxiety and improving mood in a group of adults with generalised anxiety disorder.

It can improve mood

According to a new study, focusing on the pace and timing of breath can help boost mood and direct attention. To do this, researchers conducted a study on six adults who were being monitored using an electroencephalography (EEG) device. They were asked to perform various breathing exercises, such as alternating between fast and slow breathing.

The participants were first asked to count their breaths and report how many they had taken. Then, they performed a focused task while monitoring their breath cycle. The different breathing styles activated different parts of the brain related to attention and emotion.

The study's results revealed that rapid breathing activated the amygdala, a part of the brain involved in feelings of fear and anxiety. This suggests that strategies designed to improve breathing could help people manage their emotions and thoughts.

It can improve concentration

In a study, participants who practiced mindfulness meditation showed improved performance on a test of sustained attention, compared to those in the control group. Another study found that mindfulness training was associated with increased activation in brain regions involved in attention and concentration. These findings suggest that mindfulness may help improve cognitive performance and reduce mind wandering, leading to increased focus and concentration.

It can help with ADHD

mindfulness can be a helpful tool for managing ADHD symptoms. Research has shown that mindfulness-based interventions can effectively improve symptoms of ADHD, such as inattention and hyperactivity. However, it is important to note that mindfulness should not be used as a replacement for traditional treatments for ADHD, such as medication and therapy. Working with a mental health professional to determine the best treatment plan for your individual needs is best.

It can help with OCD

OCD, or obsessive-compulsive disorder, is a mental health condition characterised by obsessive thoughts and repetitive behaviors. Mindfulness can help individuals with OCD reduce the frequency and intensity of their obsessions and compulsions by assisting them to focus on the present moment and notice their thoughts and feelings without judgment.

Mindfulness can also help manage symptoms of OCD. Research has shown that mindfulness-based interventions can be effective for reducing OCD symptoms and improving overall quality of life.

However, it is essential to note that mindfulness should not be used as a replacement for traditional treatments for OCD, such as medication and therapy. Working with a mental health professional to determine the best treatment plan for your individual needs is best.

Spiritual Benefits

There are few studies that look into the spiritual side of mindfulness, but there are plenty of reported spiritual benefits of mindfulness practice.

While mindfulness is not necessarily a spiritual practice, many people find that it has spiritual benefits. These benefits can vary depending on the individual and their personal beliefs.

One potential spiritual benefit of mindfulness is that it can help people connect with their inner selves and their spiritual beliefs.

By practicing mindfulness, people can learn to quiet their minds and focus on the present moment, allowing them to connect with their inner thoughts and feelings more profoundly. This can help people better understand their spiritual beliefs and values and connect with a sense of meaning and purpose in their lives.

Another potential spiritual benefit of mindfulness is that it can help people cultivate a sense of gratitude and appreciation for the present moment. By paying attention to the present moment and accepting it, people can learn to appreciate the beauty and goodness in their lives, even during challenges and difficulties. This can foster a sense of gratitude and contentment, which can be spiritually enriching.

Additionally, mindfulness can help people develop a sense of compassion and kindness towards themselves and others. By observing their thoughts and emotions without judgment, people can learn to be more accepting and compassionate towards themselves and others. This can foster a sense of connection and unity with others, which can be spiritually enriching.

Overall, while mindfulness is not a spiritual practice, many people do find that their mindfulness practice has spiritual benefits. These benefits can include a deeper connection with their inner selves and spiritual beliefs, a sense of gratitude and appreciation for the present moment, and a greater sense of compassion and kindness towards themselves and others.

Relationship Benefits

Studies have shown that being mindful can help predict a person's relationship satisfaction. It can also help one cope with relationship stress and improve their ability to communicate their emotions to their partner.

According to studies, being mindful can help people cope with relationship stress, improve their ability to express themselves in various social situations, and predict their relationship satisfaction.

By paying attention to the present moment and being more aware of your thoughts and emotions, you can better understand your own needs and boundaries and communicate them more effectively to your partner. This can help to reduce misunderstandings and conflicts and foster greater understanding and connection in your relationship.

Another potential relationship benefit of mindfulness is increased empathy and compassion. By practicing mindfulness, you can learn to be more aware of and accepting of your own emotions and those of your partner.

Workplace Benefits

In addition to its benefits for individuals, mindfulness has also been shown to be effective in improving the mental and physical health of groups and organisations. Mindfulness-based interventions have been used in various settings, such as schools, hospitals, and the workplace, with positive results.

For example, a study found that mindfulness training improved the mental health and well-being of students in a school setting. Another study found that mindfulness training was associated with reduced burnout and increased job satisfaction among healthcare workers. These findings suggest that mindfulness can be a valuable tool for promoting mental and physical health in various settings and groups.

The Future

Further studies are needed in some areas that show promise. For example, one 2019 study showed that mindfulness may improve mental health of people with cancer. There are other indications that it might help with weight control, eating disorders and PTSD, and ADHD (Attention-Deficit Hyperactivity Disorder).

In Summary

Beyond all of these benefits, mindfulness has also been shown to promote overall well-being. Well-being is a multidimensional construct that includes physical, mental, emotional, and social health.

In a study, participants who practiced mindfulness reported improved physical and mental health and increased happiness and life satisfaction. These findings suggest that mindfulness may have a holistic and beneficial effect on overall well-being.

In addition to its benefits for mental and physical health, mindfulness has also been shown to positively affect other aspects of life, such as relationships and personal growth. Mindfulness can help individuals develop greater self-awareness, self-compassion, and empathy, leading to improved relationships with others. It can also foster personal growth and development by promoting insight, self-reflection, and the ability to respond to challenges in a healthy and adaptive way.

In conclusion, the science of mindfulness has shown that it can be a powerful tool for promoting mental and physical health. Its wide-ranging benefits include reduced stress and anxiety, improved focus and concentration, and enhanced overall well-being. Mindfulness has been successfully used in various settings and with different populations, making it a versatile and valuable practice for promoting health and well-being. In the next chapter, we will explore how to incorporate mindfulness into daily life and overcome common challenges and obstacles to mindfulness practice.

CHAPTER FIVE

Beginning Mindfulness

TECHNIQUES AND PRACTICES

In this chapter, we will discuss some techniques and practices that can help you develop a mindfulness practice and make it a regular part of your life.

Mindfulness is not just a meditative practice, but a way of being present and aware in all aspects of your life. This chapter will discuss incorporating mindfulness into your daily activities, such as eating, walking, and interacting with others. By bringing mindfulness to these everyday activities, you can cultivate more significant presence and awareness in your daily life.

A straightforward way to practice mindfulness daily is to bring awareness to your breath and body. You can do this by taking a few moments to focus on your breath, paying attention to the sensation of the breath as it moves in and out of your body. You can also bring awareness to your body, noticing any sensations or feelings that arise. This can help to get you into the present moment and to quiet the constant stream of thoughts in your mind.

Another way to practice mindfulness daily is to bring full attention to the task at hand. This means giving your full attention to whatever you are doing, whether eating, walking, or interacting with others. For example, when eating, you can focus on your food's taste, texture, and appearance and savour each bite. When walking, you can pay attention to the sensation of your feet on the ground and the sights and sounds around you. And when interacting with others, you can listen actively and without judgment and respond with kindness and empathy.

Practising mindfulness in daily life can be challenging, as the mind is naturally inclined to wander and get caught up in thoughts and worries. But with regular practice, you can develop greater focus and concentration, and bring mindfulness to your daily activities more efficiently.

Try the following exercises to get started. There's no rush, try each one at a time. Play with it, explore it, and don't feel a sense of pressure or urgency as you do. These aren't tasks to be checked off a to-do list but practices you will hopefully incorporate into the rest of your life.

The Raisin Exercise

This is a classic exercise from a well-respected mindfulness training program, developed by two well known practitioners.

The raisin exercise is a mindfulness practice that involves paying close attention to the sensation of eating a raisin. This exercise can help you to improve focus and concentration by bringing attention to the present moment and noticing the sensations of eating without judgment.

To do the raisin exercise, you will need a raisin. Take a moment to look at the raisin, noticing its color, texture, and shape. Take a deep breath and bring your attention to the present moment. Then, pick up the raisin and hold it in your hand. Notice the weight and texture of the raisin, and the way it feels in your hand. Slowly bring the raisin to your mouth and take a small bite. Chew the raisin slowly, noticing the taste and texture of the raisin. Notice the way the raisin feels in your mouth, and the sensation of swallowing. Continue to focus on the sensation of eating the raisin until it is gone. This exercise can help to improve your focus and concentration, and can also help to reduce stress and anxiety.

Non-guided breath focus

Non-guided breath focus is a mindfulness practice that focuses on the sensation of the breath without using a guided meditation. This practice can help individuals to improve their focus and concentration by bringing their attention to the present moment and letting go of distractions.

To do a non-guided breath focus, find a comfortable seated position and close your eyes. Take a few deep breaths to relax and focus your mind. Then, bring your attention to the sensation of the breath, noticing the way it moves in and out of the body. Notice the sensation of the breath as it enters and exits the nostrils, and the way the chest and abdomen rise and fall with each breath. As you continue to focus on the breath, imagine that you are gradually becoming more and more relaxed and calm. Allow any distractions or thoughts that come up to pass by, and continue to focus on the breath. When you are ready, slowly open your eyes. This practice can help to improve your focus and concentration, and can also help to reduce stress and anxiety.

Mindful Breathing

This is a simpler version of non-guided breath focus - mindful breathing involves paying attention to the breath as it moves in and out of the body. This can be done by sitting comfortably and focusing on the sensation of the breath entering and leaving the nose or mouth. It can also involve counting each breath, or using a specific word or phrase to focus the mind, such as "in" and "out" or "peace" and "calm." Mindful breathing can be done for a few minutes at a time, and can be practiced at any time of day.

Mindful Seeing

Mindfulness seeing exercise is a type of mindfulness practice that involves paying attention to the act of seeing. This exercise can help individuals to improve their focus and concentration by bringing their attention to the present moment and noticing the sights around them without judgment. To do a mindfulness seeing exercise, you can sit in a comfortable position and close your eyes. Take a few deep breaths to relax and focus your mind. Then, open your eyes and look around the room. Notice the colors, shapes, and textures of the objects in the room. Try to notice details that you may not have noticed before. Notice how your eyes move from one thing to another, and how the objects in the room appear and disappear in your field of vision. Notice any judgments or thoughts that come up, and let them pass without getting caught up in them. Continue to focus on the act of seeing for a few minutes, and then take a few deep breaths and slowly open your eyes. This exercise can help to improve your focus and concentration, and can also help to reduce stress and anxiety.

Mindful Listening

Mindful listening is a mindfulness practice that involves paying attention to the act of listening. This practice can help individuals to improve their focus and concentration by bringing their attention to the present moment and noticing the sounds around them without judgment. To do a mindful listening exercise, find a quiet place where you can sit comfortably and close your eyes. Take a few deep breaths to relax and focus your mind. Then, begin to listen to the sounds around you, noticing the different sounds and how they change over time. Notice the quality of the sounds, such as whether they are high or low, loud or soft, smooth or rough. Notice any judgments or thoughts that come up, and let them pass without getting caught up in them. Continue to focus on the act of listening for a few minutes, and then take a few deep breaths and slowly open your eyes.

Body Scan

A body scan involves paying attention to physical sensations in the body, such as tension or discomfort, and you do so by focusing your attention on different parts of your body, one at a time, to increase awareness of your physical sensations.

To do a body scan, you can lie down on your back or sit comfortably in a chair with your feet firmly planted on the ground. Then, starting at your feet, slowly bring your attention to each part of your body, noticing any sensations that are present, such as warmth, tingling, or pressure. As you move up through your body, try to let go of any judgments or evaluations about the sensations you are feeling, and simply observe them with curiosity.

You can use this list to move your focus:

Toes of both feet, the whole of your feet, your knees, lower legs, thighs, abdomen, upper back, chest, hands, upper and lower back, elbows, forehead, nose, mouth, and cheeks.

The body scan can take anywhere from 10 to 45 minutes, depending on how much time you have and how comfortable you are with the practice. It can be a helpful way to relax and destress, and can also help to improve your body awareness and overall well-being.

Mindful Movement

Mindful movement involves bringing awareness to the body as it moves, such as in yoga or tai chi. This can involve paying attention to the breath and the sensations in the body as the body moves through various postures or sequences. Mindful movement can be a relaxing and energising practice, and can be done for a few minutes at a time or for longer periods.

3-Minute Breathing Space

The 3-minute breathing space exercise is a mindfulness practice that involves taking a brief pause to focus on the breath and the present moment. This practice can help individuals to improve their focus and concentration and to manage stress and anxiety in the moment. The 3-minute breathing space exercise consists of three steps:

1. Pause: Take a moment to pause and become aware of the present moment. Notice any judgments or thoughts that come up, and let them pass without getting caught up in them.

2. Focus on the breath: Bring your attention to the sensation of the breath, noticing the way the

breath moves in and out of the body. Notice the sensation of the breath as it enters and exits the nostrils, and the way the chest and abdomen rise and fall with each breath.

3. Expand your awareness: Slowly expand your awareness to include your body and your surroundings. Notice any sensations in your body, and the sights, sounds, and other sensations around you. Notice any judgments or thoughts that come up, and let them pass without getting caught up in them.

This exercise can be done in just a few minutes, and can be helpful when you are feeling stressed or overwhelmed.

Mindfulness of the Senses

Mindfulness of the senses, also known as mindfulness of the five senses, is a type of mindfulness practice in which you focus your attention on each of your five senses – sight, sound, smell, taste, and touch – to increase awareness of your sensory experience. To do this practice, find a comfortable and quiet place to sit or lie down. Then, bring your attention to each of your five senses, one at a time, and notice any sensations that are present. For example, if you are focusing on your sense of sight, you might notice the colors and shapes of the objects around you. If you are focusing on your sense of sound, you might notice the sounds of traffic or birds outside. If you are focusing on your sense of smell, you might notice the smell of flowers or food. The key is to simply notice what is happening in the present moment, without judging or evaluating it. This practice can help to improve your awareness of your sensory experience, and can also be a helpful way to reduce stress and increase relaxation.

The Three-Step Mindfulness Exercise

The 3-step mindfulness exercise is a simple mindfulness practice that involves paying attention to the present moment in three steps. This exercise can help individuals to improve their focus and concentration by bringing their attention to the present moment and letting go of distractions. The three steps of the exercise are as follows:

1. Pay attention to your breath: Bring your attention to the sensation of the breath, noticing the way the breath moves in and out of the body. Notice

the sensation of the breath as it enters and exits the nostrils, and the way the chest and abdomen rise and fall with each breath.

2. Notice your surroundings: Bring your attention to the sights, sounds, and other sensations around you, noticing the details of your environment without judgment. Notice the colors, shapes, and textures of objects in your environment, and the sounds you hear, such as the sound of traffic, birds, or the wind.

3. Be aware of your thoughts and emotions: Bring your attention to your thoughts and emotions, noticing them without judgment. Notice the quality of your thoughts and emotions, such as whether they are positive or negative, and the way they make you feel. Allow any distractions or thoughts that come up to pass by, and continue to focus on the present moment.

By practicing this exercise regularly, you can improve your focus and concentration, and reduce stress and anxiety.

Mindful Eating

Mindful eating is a mindfulness practice that involves paying attention to the act of eating and the sensations of hunger and fullness. This practice can help individuals to improve their focus and concentration, and to develop a healthier relationship with food. To do a mindful eating exercise, find a quiet place where you can sit comfortably and prepare a small snack or meal. Take a moment to look at the food, noticing its color, texture, and smell. Take a few deep breaths to relax and focus your mind. Then, begin to eat slowly and mindfully, noticing the taste and texture of each bite. Notice the sensations of hunger and fullness in your body, and stop eating when you feel satisfied. Notice any judgments or thoughts that come up, and let them pass without getting caught up in them. Continue to focus on the act of eating and the sensations of hunger and fullness for the duration of the meal. This exercise can help to improve your focus and concentration, and can also help to reduce stress and anxiety. It is important to note that mindful eating should be done slowly and mindfully, and not as a way to restrict or control your food intake.

Mindfulness in Daily Activities

In addition to meditation, mindfulness can also be incorporated into daily activities, such as eating, walking, and doing chores. This is known as "informal" mindfulness practice, and it involves bringing a mindful awareness to whatever you are doing in the present moment. For example, when you are eating, you can try to focus on the colors, textures, and flavors of the food, and notice any sensations or thoughts that arise. When you are walking, you can try to pay attention to the sensations of your feet on the ground and the sights, sounds, and smells around you. When you are doing chores, you can try to be fully present and aware of what you are doing, without getting lost in your thoughts or distractions.

Sure, mindfulness is a mental state that involves bringing your attention to the present moment and accepting it without judgment. It is a way of paying attention to your thoughts and feelings in a non-judgmental way. Here are a few mindfulness techniques that you can try:

• Take a few deep breaths and focus on the sensation of the breath as it enters and leaves your body. This can help to ground you in the present moment and calm your mind.

• Pay attention to your surroundings and notice the colors, sounds, and smells that are present. This can help to increase your awareness and improve your concentration.

• Notice any judgments or thoughts that come into your mind and try to let them pass without getting caught up in them. This can help to increase your awareness and improve your ability to let go of unhelpful thoughts.

• Engage in a physical activity, such as yoga or walking, and focus on the sensation of your body moving and your breath. This can help to improve your body awareness and increase your mindfulness.

• Try to be present in each moment and avoid getting caught up in thoughts about the past or future. This can help to improve your ability to be mindful in your daily life.

• Practice gratitude by taking a few moments to think about the things that you are grateful for in your life. This can help to improve your mood and increase your sense of well-being.

Journaling

Journaling can be a helpful tool for cultivating mindfulness because it allows you to reflect on their thoughts, feelings, and experiences in a structured and intentional way. By regularly writing in a journal, you can develop the ability to notice thoughts and emotions without getting caught up in them. This can help to improve focus and concentration, and to reduce stress and anxiety. In addition, journaling can provide a sense of clarity and insight, and can help you to gain a better understanding of their thoughts, feelings, and behaviors. To use journaling for mindfulness, you can set aside some time each day to write in a journal. You can start by writing about your thoughts and feelings in the present moment, and then reflect on your experiences throughout the day. You can also write about any insights or observations that come up during your journaling practice. It is important to approach journaling with an open and curious mind, and to avoid judging or criticising your thoughts and feelings.

Mindful Gardening

Mindful gardening is a mindfulness practice that involves bringing your attention to the present moment while engaging in the activity of gardening. This practice can help individuals to improve their focus and concentration, and to cultivate a sense of calm and connection with nature. To do a mindful gardening exercise, find a quiet place where you can engage in gardening activities, such as planting seeds or tending to plants. Take a few deep breaths to relax and focus your mind. Then, begin to engage in gardening activities, noticing the sensations and movements of your body as you work. Notice the sights, sounds, and other sensations of the garden, and allow any judgments or thoughts that come up to pass by without getting caught up in them. Continue to focus on the present moment and the sensations of gardening for the duration of the activity. This exercise can help to improve your focus and concentration, and can also help to reduce stress and anxiety. It is important to note that mindful gardening should be done slowly and mindfully, and not as a way to accomplish tasks or goals.

These are just a few examples of mindfulness techniques. The important thing is to find a technique that works for you and to practice it regularly in order to improve your mindfulness.

Overall, the best mindfulness technique is the one that resonates with you and that you are able to stick with over time. It may take some experimentation to find the right technique for you, but the important thing is to keep practicing and stay committed to the process.

Incorporating mindfulness into daily life can be challenging, and it may take some time to develop a regular practice. It can be helpful to set aside a specific time each day for mindfulness practice, and to find a comfortable and quiet space to practice. It can also be helpful to seek support and guidance from a trained mindfulness teacher or practitioner.

CHAPTER SIX

Beginning Meditation

One of the key components of mindfulness is the practice of meditation. Meditation is a mental training technique that involves focusing the mind on a single object, such as the breath, a sound, or a phrase, and letting go of thoughts and distractions. It is often used as a tool for mindfulness, which involves paying attention to the present moment and noticing thoughts and feelings without judgment.

There are many different types of meditation, but they all involve developing a heightened awareness of the present moment and a non-judgmental attitude towards one's thoughts and experiences.

To begin a mindfulness meditation practice, you can try the following mindfulness practice:

1. Find a comfortable seated position, with your back straight and your feet firmly planted on the ground.

2. Take a few deep breaths, and allow your body to relax.

3. Bring your attention to your breath, and notice the sensation of the breath as it moves in and out of your body.

4. Notice any thoughts, feelings, or sensations that arise, and let them be without judgment or attachment.

5. When your mind wanders, gently bring your attention back to your breath.

6. Continue with this practice for a few minutes, or longer if you wish.

Mountain Meditation

Another form of meditation often used in mindfulness training is 'mountain meditation'. This mindfulness practice involves focusing on the image of a mountain to cultivate a sense of calm and stillness. This meditation can help individuals to improve their focus and concentration by bringing their attention to the present moment and letting go of distractions. To do a mountain meditation, find a comfortable seated position and close your eyes. Take a few deep breaths to relax and focus your mind. Imagine that you are standing at the base of a mountain. Notice the size and shape of the mountain, and the way it feels to be in its presence. Notice the color and texture of the mountain, and any other details that come to mind. As you continue to focus on the mountain, imagine that you are gradually becoming more and more still and calm, like the mountain itself. Allow any distractions or thoughts that come up to pass by, and continue to focus on the mountain. When you are ready, slowly open your eyes.

Lake Meditation

In a similar vein, lake meditation is a mindfulness practice that involves focusing on the image of a calm and peaceful lake to cultivate a sense of relaxation and tranquility. This meditation can help individuals to improve their focus and concentration by bringing their attention to the present moment and letting go of distractions. To do a lake meditation, sit comfortably and close your eyes. Take a few deep breaths to relax and focus your mind. Imagine that you are standing by the edge of a calm and peaceful lake. Notice the color and texture of the water, and the way the sunlight reflects off the lake's surface. Notice the sounds of the water, the gentle breeze, and how they make you feel. As you focus on the lake, imagine that you are gradually becoming more relaxed and peaceful, like the lake itself. Allow any distractions or thoughts to pass by, and continue to focus on the lake. When you are ready, slowly open your eyes.

Observer Meditation

Observer meditation is a mindfulness practice that involves becoming an observer of your thoughts and feelings without getting caught up in them. This practice can help individuals to improve their focus and concentration by bringing their attention to the present moment and letting go of distractions. To do an observer meditation, find a comfortable seated position and close your eyes. Take a few deep breaths to relax and focus your mind. Then, bring your attention to your thoughts and feelings, noticing them without judgment. Imagine you are an observer, watching your thoughts and feelings as they arise and pass away. Notice the quality of your thoughts and feelings, such as positive or negative, and how they make you feel. Allow any distractions or thoughts that come up to pass by, and continue to observe your thoughts and feelings without getting caught up in them. When you are ready, slowly open your eyes.

Walking Meditation

Walking meditation is a mindfulness practice that involves bringing your attention to the sensation of walking and the present moment. This practice can help individuals to improve their focus and concentration by letting go of distractions and bringing their attention to the present moment. To do a walking meditation, find a quiet place where you can walk comfortably and slowly. Begin by standing still, with your feet hip-width apart and your arms relaxed by your sides. Take a few deep breaths to relax and focus your mind. Then, begin to walk slowly, noticing the sensation of each step as your foot touches the ground. Notice the way your body moves and feels as you walk, and the way the ground feels beneath your feet. Notice the sights, sounds, and other sensations around you, and allow any judgments or thoughts that come up to pass by without getting caught up in them. Continue to focus on the sensation of walking and the present moment for a few minutes, and then stop and stand still again. Close your eyes, take a few deep breaths, and slowly open your eyes. This meditation can help to improve your focus and concentration, and can also help to reduce stress and anxiety. It is important to note that walking meditation should be done slowly and mindfully, and not as a form of exercise or physical activity.

CHAPTER SEVEN

Overcoming Challenges

HOW TO REMAIN CONSISTENT

In the previous chapter, we discussed the techniques and practices that can help you incorporate mindfulness into daily life. However, as with any skill or habit, mindfulness can be challenging to develop and maintain. In this chapter, we will explore some common challenges and obstacles to mindfulness in more detail, and offer suggestions for overcoming them.

Lack of Motivation

One of the most common obstacles to mindfulness practice is lack of motivation. Finding the time and energy to practice mindfulness regularly can be difficult, especially when faced with competing demands and distractions. There may be many reasons why you might not feel motivated to practice mindfulness, such as feeling overwhelmed, stressed, or bored. To overcome this obstacle, it is important to remind yourself of the benefits of mindfulness and why it is worth the effort. You can also try to make mindfulness practice a priority by setting aside a specific time and place for it every day, and sticking to it as much as possible.

Difficulty Concentrating

Another common challenge to mindfulness is difficulty concentrating. Our minds naturally wander and get lost in thoughts and distractions. This can make it difficult to focus on the present moment and be aware of our thoughts and sensations. The constant stream of stimuli and information we are exposed to daily life can also make it difficult to quiet the mind and be mindful. It is important to be patient and persistent with your mindfulness practice to overcome this challenge. Remember that mindfulness is a skill that takes time and practice to develop, and it is normal to experience setbacks and difficulties. You can also try using techniques, such as focusing on the breath or a mantra, to help you stay focused and bring your attention back to the present moment when it wanders.

Presence of Negative Thoughts and Emotions

Another obstacle to mindfulness practice is the presence of negative thoughts and emotions. It is natural to experience negative thoughts and emotions from time to time, and mindfulness does not involve getting rid of them or pretending they don't exist. However, these thoughts and emotions can be uncomfortable and distracting, and it can be difficult to be mindful when we are caught up in them. It is important to approach negative thoughts and emotions with curiosity and compassion to overcome this obstacle. Instead of judging or resisting them, try to observe them with an open mind and a kind heart. Notice where they arise in the body, and how they change and pass. This can help you develop a greater sense of distance and perspective, and reduce their power and influence over you.

One common challenge that people may face when starting a mindfulness practice is difficulty focusing and letting go of distracting thoughts. The mind is naturally inclined to wander, and it can be difficult to quiet the constant stream of thoughts and stay focused on the present moment. This can make it hard to get started with mindfulness and cause some people to give up on the practice.

It is important to be patient and persistent with your mindfulness practice to overcome this challenge. Don't expect to be able to quiet your mind completely, or to never have distracting thoughts. Instead, focus on bringing your attention back to the present moment whenever you notice that your mind has wandered. Over time, with regular practice, you will develop greater focus and concentration, and your ability to let go of distracting thoughts will improve.

Finding Time

In addition to these common challenges and obstacles, other factors may make it difficult for you to practice mindfulness. For example, you may have a busy schedule, a chronic illness, or other responsibilities that limit your ability to practice regularly. It is important to be realistic and flexible in your approach to mindfulness, and to find ways to incorporate it into your life that work for you. For example, you can try short and simple mindfulness exercises, such as taking a few mindful breaths or noticing the sensations in your body, throughout the day. You can also try to be mindful in your daily activities, such as eating, walking, or doing chores.

Attitude and Mindset

Another factor that can affect your ability to practice mindfulness is your attitude and mindset. If you approach mindfulness with a negative or skeptical attitude, engaging in the practice and reap its benefits can be difficult. To overcome this obstacle, it is important to cultivate a positive and curious mindset. Mindfulness is not about achieving perfection or getting rid of negative thoughts and emotions. It is about being present and accepting whatever arises in the moment, with kindness and curiosity. By adopting a positive and open attitude towards mindfulness, you can increase your enjoyment and engagement in the practice, and enhance its benefits for your mental and physical health.

Starting a mindfulness practice can be challenging, and it is common to encounter obstacles and challenges along the way. In this chapter, we will discuss some of these challenges and offer tips and strategies for overcoming them and staying committed to your mindfulness practice.

Feeling Overwhelmed

Another challenge that people may face when starting a mindfulness practice is feeling overwhelmed or uncomfortable. Some mindfulness practices, such as body scan or mindful breathing, can bring up difficult emotions or sensations in the body. This can be challenging and even uncomfortable, and can cause some people to avoid or resist these practices.

To overcome this challenge, it is important to approach your mindfulness practice with a sense of curiosity and openness. Try to cultivate a non-judgmental attitude towards your emotions and sensations, and allow yourself to experience them without trying to push them away. Over time, with regular practice, you will develop a greater ability to tolerate and even embrace difficult emotions and sensations, and they will become less overwhelming.

Inconsistency

Another challenge that people may face when starting a mindfulness practice is inconsistency and lack of commitment. It can be easy to get caught up in daily life's demands and neglect your mindfulness practice.

To overcome this challenge, it is important to prioritise your mindfulness practice and make it a regular part of your routine. Set aside a specific time for mindfulness practice each day, and commit to stick to this schedule. You can also try to incorporate mindfulness into your daily activities, such as eating, walking, and interacting with others. By making mindfulness a regular part of your life, you will be more likely to stay committed to the practice.

Making Technology an Ally

Technology can be either an ally or an enemy in the quest for mindfulness. If used well, it will help you. If you let it control you (as many apps and software are designed to do), then mindfulness will become harder to achieve.

Here are some tips to consider:

1. Use technology to set boundaries: Many smartphones and other devices have built-in tools that can help you manage your screen time and set limits on how much time you spend on certain apps or websites. For example, you can use the "Screen Time" feature on iOS devices or the "Digital Wellbeing" feature on Android devices to set limits on how much time you spend on your phone each day, or to limit the use of specific apps during certain times of the day.

2. Use technology to support mindfulness practices: Many apps and websites, such as Headspace and Calm, can help you practice mindfulness and meditation. These apps can guide mindfulness techniques and help

you stay focused and calm during meditation.

3. Use technology to stay organised and reduce stress: Technology can be used to help you stay organised and reduce stress by keeping track of your to-do lists, scheduling reminders, and managing your time effectively. For example, you can use a calendar app to keep track of important deadlines and appointments, or a task management app to help you stay on top of your to-do list.

4. Take regular breaks from technology: it's important to unplug and disconnect from technology on a regular basis. Taking regular breaks from screens can help you recharge and refocus, and can also help reduce the negative effects of excessive screen time. For example, you could set aside specific times each day when you will not use any technology or take a "digital detox" by going on a technology-free vacation or retreat.

General Tips

Here are some tips for overcoming common obstacles to mindfulness practice:

- Set realistic goals and expectations for your mindfulness practice. Don't try to do too much too soon, and remember that progress is not always linear.

- Be consistent and regular with your practice. Try to set aside a specific time and place for mindfulness every day, and stick to it as much as possible.

- Use reminders and cues to help you stay focused. For example, tk

- Use reminders and cues to help you stay focused. For example, you can set an alarm on your phone to remind you to practice mindfulness, or you can use a small object, such as a stone or a bracelet, as a physical reminder to be mindful.

- Seek support and guidance from others. Mindfulness is a journey that is best traveled with others. You can join a mindfulness group, attend a workshop or retreat, or work with a teacher or therapist who can provide guidance and support.

- Cultivate a positive attitude and a non-judgmental mindset. Mindfulness is not about achieving perfection or getting rid of negative thoughts and emotions. It is about being present and accepting whatever arises in the moment, with kindness and curiosity.

In conclusion, mindfulness practice can be challenging, but it is worth the effort. By overcoming common obstacles and challenges, you can develop a regular and consistent mindfulness practice, and reap the benefits of increased awareness, clarity, and well-being. In the next chapter, we will explore how mindfulness has been used in various settings, and discuss its potential applications in promoting health and well-being.

CHAPTER EIGHT

Mindfulness for Everyone

ANYONE CAN CHANGE THEIR LIFE

Mindfulness has been used in various settings, including schools, hospitals, and the workplace.

Education

In schools, mindfulness-based interventions have been shown to improve students' mental health and well-being. A study found that mindfulness training improved the mental health and well-being of students in a school setting. The study involved a group of middle school students who participated in a mindfulness-based intervention program over a period of six weeks. The students showed significant improvements in their mental health and well-being, as measured by self-report questionnaires and interviews. The study suggests that mindfulness can be a valuable tool for promoting students' mental health and well-being, and for improving the learning environment in schools.

Healthcare

In hospitals and healthcare settings, mindfulness has been used to reduce burnout and improve job satisfaction among healthcare workers. A study found that mindfulness training was associated with reduced burnout and increased job satisfaction among healthcare workers. The study involved a group of healthcare workers who participated in a mindfulness-based intervention program over eight weeks. The workers showed significant improvements in their burnout and job satisfaction, as measured by self-report questionnaires and interviews. The study suggests that mindfulness can be a valuable tool for promoting healthcare workers' mental and physical health and improving patient care quality.

Workplace

In the workplace, mindfulness has been used to reduce stress and improve job performance. A study found mindfulness training was associated with reduced job stress and increased employee performance. The study involved a group of employees who participated in a mindfulness-based intervention program over eight weeks. The employees showed significant improvements in their job stress and performance, as measured by self-report questionnaires and objective measures. The study suggests that mindfulness can be a valuable tool for promoting employees' mental and physical health, and for improving organisations' overall performance and well-being.

Mental Health

In addition to its benefits for individuals and groups, mindfulness has also been used to address specific mental health conditions, such as anxiety, depression, and addiction. A study published in the journal JAMA Psychiatry found that mindfulness-based cognitive therapy (MBCT) effectively reduced the risk of relapse in patients with recurrent depression. The study involved a group of patients with a history of recurrent depression and who participated in an MBCT program over eight weeks. The patients showed significant reductions in the risk of relapse, as measured by self-report questionnaires and clinical assessments. The study suggests that mindfulness can be a valuable tool for addressing specific mental health conditions and improving individuals' overall well-being (see chapter 4 for more details).

In conclusion, mindfulness has the potential to make a significant impact in various settings and with different populations. Its wide-ranging benefits include reduced stress and anxiety, improved focus and concentration, and enhanced overall well-being. As research continues to grow and support the effectiveness of mindfulness-based interventions, there is great potential for mindfulness to become an integral part of healthcare, education, and the workplace, and to improve the lives of individuals and communities.

CHAPTER NINE

Advanced Mindfulness

Once you have established a regular mindfulness practice and understand the basics well, you may be ready to explore more advanced mindfulness techniques and applications. This chapter will discuss some of these advanced practices and how they can help you deepen your mindfulness experience.

Loving Kindness Meditation

One advanced mindfulness practice is loving-kindness meditation. This practice involves focusing on feelings of love and compassion for oneself and others, and can be a powerful tool for cultivating empathy, kindness, and forgiveness. To practice loving-kindness meditation, you can repeat phrases such as "may I be happy, may I be healthy, may I be at peace" to yourself, and then extend these phrases to others, such as friends, family, and even those who may have caused you harm.

Loving-kindness meditation can be challenging, as it may bring up difficult emotions and thoughts. However, regular practice can help cultivate a more compassionate and open-hearted attitude towards yourself and others. It can also help reduce anger, resentment, and jealousy and cultivate a sense of connection and belonging.

Daily Life Mindfulness

We talked about this in the 'Beginning Mindfulness' chapter, but the truth is that integrating mindfulness in your daily life is one of the hardest things to do. During meditation, and other forms of mindfulness, we can have the luxury of being in a quiet, calm environment. When we're trying to practice mindfulness in daily life, we're doing it surrounded by chaotic events and people.

To practice mindfulness in daily life, you can start by bringing awareness to your breath and body as you go about your daily activities. For example, as you brush your teeth in the morning, you can focus on the sensation of the toothbrush on your teeth and the taste of the toothpaste in your mouth. As you walk to work, you can pay attention to the sensation of your feet on the ground and the sights and sounds around you. By bringing mindfulness to these everyday activities, you can start to cultivate greater presence and awareness in your daily life.

Mindfulness can also be applied in various settings and contexts, such as at work, in relationships, and for managing physical and emotional health. For example, mindfulness can be useful in managing stress and improving communication and collaboration in the workplace. By bringing mindfulness to your work tasks, you can improve your focus and productivity, and reduce the negative impact of stress on your well-being.

Relationships

In relationships, mindfulness can help to reduce conflicts and enhance connection and intimacy. By practicing mindfulness in your interactions with others, you can improve your communication and listening skills, and cultivate a greater understanding and empathy for others. This can help to reduce misunderstandings and conflicts, and to build stronger, more fulfilling relationships.

To Help with Pain

For physical and emotional health, mindfulness can be used to manage chronic pain, anxiety, and other conditions. By bringing mindfulness to your body and emotions, you can learn to better manage your physical and emotional responses to stress and pain, and to cultivate a sense of calm and well-being.

CHAPTER TEN

Mindfulness Overview

COME BACK TO HERE WHEN YOU'RE OVERWHELMED

Mindfulness is the practice of bringing your attention to the present moment and letting go of distracting thoughts and emotions.

This is all you need to do to practice mindfulness:

1. Start by setting aside a few minutes each day to focus on your breath or an object or activity. This can be as simple as watching your breath go in and out, or as complex as focusing on a difficult puzzle.

2. Try to maintain a non-judgmental attitude

as you focus on the present moment. This means letting go of thoughts like "this is good" or "this is bad," and simply noticing what is happening without reacting to it.

3. If your mind starts to wander, gently bring your attention back to the present moment. This is a natural part of the process, and it's important to be kind to yourself as you practice.

4. Over time, you can try incorporating mindfulness into your daily activities, such as eating, walking, or even working. This can help you to stay present and focused throughout the day.

5. Remember that mindfulness is a skill that takes time and practice to develop. Be patient with yourself and keep coming back to the present moment, even when it's difficult.

CHAPTER ELEVEN

Mindfulness FAQ

What is mindfulness?

Mindfulness is the practice of bringing one's attention to the present moment and being aware of one's thoughts, feelings, and surroundings. It is a mental state characterised by focusing on the present moment and accepting one's thoughts and feelings without judgment. The goal of mindfulness is to cultivate a greater sense of awareness and presence, and to improve mental and emotional well-being.

How do I practice mindfulness?

To practice mindfulness, you can try focusing your attention on your breath or on a specific object, such as a candle flame or a mantra. You can also try paying attention to your senses, such as the sensations of touch, taste, sight, sound, and smell. Another way to practice mindfulness is to engage in activities that require focus and concentration, such as coloring or drawing, knitting or crochet, or doing puzzles or crosswords. You can also try incorporating mindfulness into your daily activities by paying attention to your thoughts and feelings while eating or showering.

What are the benefits of mindfulness?

The benefits of mindfulness include reduced stress and anxiety, improved focus and concentration, increased emotional well-being, and better physical health. Mindfulness can also help to reduce negative thought patterns and improve overall mental well-being.

Is mindfulness the same as meditation?

Mindfulness and meditation are related, but they are not the same thing. Meditation is a specific practice involving focusing the mind on a specific object or sensation, such as the breath, to cultivate mindfulness. On the other hand, mindfulness is the mental state of being aware of and present in the moment, and can be practiced in many different ways, including through meditation.

Is mindfulness only for adults?

No, mindfulness is not only for adults. While mindfulness can be particularly beneficial for adults, it can also be helpful for children and teenagers. Mindfulness can help children develop greater focus and attention, improving their overall well-being. There is no age limit to practicing mindfulness; anyone can benefit from it.

Does mindfulness require a lot of time?

No, mindfulness does not necessarily require a lot of time to practice. While it is true that some mindfulness exercises, such as formal meditation, can take longer, mindfulness can also be incorporated into everyday activities and can be practiced for just a few minutes at a time.

How can mindfulness help with stress and anxiety?

Mindfulness can help with stress and anxiety by teaching you to be more present and aware of your thoughts and feelings. By practicing mindfulness, you can learn to recognise when you are getting caught up in negative thought patterns and to let go of them without getting caught up in them. Mindfulness can also help you to respond to stress and anxiety in a more balanced and measured way, rather than reacting automatically or impulsively.

Can mindfulness be practiced in everyday life?

Yes, mindfulness can be practiced in everyday life. You can try incorporating mindfulness into your daily activities by paying attention to your thoughts and feelings while eating or showering. You can also try practicing mindfulness during activities that require focus and concentration, such as coloring or drawing, knitting or crochet, or doing puzzles or crosswords.

Is mindfulness a form of religion or spirituality?

Mindfulness is not inherently tied to any particular religion or belief system. While mindfulness is often used as a part of meditation and can be a spiritual practice for some people, it can be practiced by people of any faith or belief system, or by those who do not follow any specific religion.

Chapter Twelve

Conclusion

THE FUTURE OF MINDFULNESS AND ITS ROLE IN PROMOTING WELL-BEING

In the previous chapters, we discussed the benefits of mindfulness and how it has been used in various settings and with different populations. In this chapter, we will explore the future of mindfulness and its potential role in promoting health and well-being.

The future of mindfulness looks bright, as more and more research supports its effectiveness in promoting mental and physical health. As research continues to grow and expand, there is great potential for mindfulness to become an integral part of the healthcare and education systems and the workplace. In addition, there is growing interest in mindfulness-based interventions for specific mental health conditions, such as anxiety, depression, and addiction.

One of the key areas where mindfulness has the potential to make a significant impact is in the field of mental health. With the increasing prevalence of mental health conditions, such as anxiety and depression, there is a growing need for effective interventions that can help individuals manage their symptoms and improve their overall well-being. Mindfulness-based interventions, such as MBSR and MBCT, are effective in reducing symptoms of anxiety and depression and preventing relapse in individuals with recurrent depression. These interventions are relatively low-cost and can be delivered in various settings, including schools, hospitals, and the workplace. As such, mindfulness has the potential to become a valuable tool in the mental health field, and to improve the lives of millions of individuals.

Another area where mindfulness has the potential to make a significant impact is in the workplace. With the increasing demands and pressures of modern work, there is a growing need for interventions that can help employees manage stress and improve their performance and well-being. Mindfulness-based interventions have been shown to be effective in reducing job stress and improving job performance among employees. These interventions can be easily integrated into the workplace and delivered in various formats, including group classes, workshops, and online courses. As such, mindfulness has the potential to become an integral part of workplace wellness programs, and to improve the overall performance and well-being of organisations.

In addition to its potential benefits for individuals and groups, mindfulness also has the potential to make a positive impact on society as a whole. By promoting mental and physical health, mindfulness can help reduce healthcare costs and improve productivity and quality of your life.

I wish you all the best in your mindfulness journey.

CHAPTER THIRTEEN

Resources

You don't need much to start your journey to a more mindful life. In fact, you don't need anything at all. Sometimes, though, some support is welcome.

With that in mind, here are some items that can help.

Websites

Many great websites offer information and resources on mindfulness. Some of the best include:

1. The Center for Mindfulness at the Universi-

ty of Massachusetts (https://www.umassm ed.edu/cfm/): This is the official website of the Center for Mindfulness, which is a leading organization in the field of mindfulness research and practice. The website offers a variety of resources, including information on mindfulness-based programs, research, and events.

2. Mindful.org   (https://www.mindful.org/) : This is the official website of Mindful magazine, which is a leading publication in the field of mindfulness. The website offers a wealth of information and resources on mindfulness, including articles, videos, and guided meditations.

3. The Mindfulness-Based Stress Reduction (MBSR) program (https://www.mindfulne sscds.com/): This website offers information on the MBSR program, which is a widely-used mindfulness-based program for reducing stress and improving well-being. The website includes information on the program, and resources for finding an MBSR course near you.

4. The Mindfulness Association (https://ww

w.mindfulnessassociation.net/): This is the official website of the Mindfulness Association, a UK-based organization that offers mindfulness training and certification. The website offers a variety of resources on mindfulness, including articles, courses, and events.

Podcasts

There are many great podcasts available on the topic of mindfulness. Some of the best include:

1. "10% Happier with Dan Harris" (https://www.10percenthappier.com/podcast): This podcast is hosted by journalist Dan Harris and features interviews with experts in the field of mindfulness and meditation, as well as practical advice and guidance on how to cultivate mindfulness in daily life.

2. "The Mindful Minute" (https://www.tenpercent.com/mindful-minute): This podcast is produced by the team behind the 10% Happier app and offers short, daily mindfulness

exercises that can be done in just a few minutes.

3. "Meditation Oasis" (https://www.meditatio noasis.com/podcasts/): This podcast offers a variety of guided meditation and mindfulness exercises, as well as discussions on mindfulness-related topics.

4. "The Mindfulness Show" (https://www.th emindfulnessshow.com/): This podcast is hosted by mindfulness teacher and author Dr. Elisha Goldstein and offers interviews with experts in the field of mindfulness, as well as practical advice and guidance for incorporating mindfulness into daily life.

5. "Mindful in Minutes" (https://www.heads pace.com/podcasts): This podcast is produced by the team behind the Headspace app and offers short mindfulness exercises that can be done in just a few minutes, as well as discussions on mindfulness-related topics.

Apps

There are many great apps available for learning and practising mindfulness. Here are five of the best

1. Headspace (https://www.headspace.com/) : Headspace is a popular app that offers a variety of mindfulness and meditation exercises, and resources for stress and sleep management.

2. Calm (https://www.calm.com/): Calm is another popular app that offers a wide range of mindfulness and meditation exercises, sleep stories and music to help users relax and unwind.

3. Insight Timer (https://insighttimer.com/) : Insight Timer is a free app that offers a large library of mindfulness and meditation exercises, and a social community for users to connect with others and share their experiences.

4. 10% Happier (https://www.10percenthappier.com/): 10% Happier is an app that offers a variety of mindfulness and meditation exercises, access to live events and discussions with experts in the field.

5. Smiling Mind (https://www.smilingmind.com.au/): Smiling Mind is a free app that offers a range of mindfulness and meditation exercises for users of all ages, and resources for educators and parents.

Journals

As we looked at in Chapter 5, using a journal can help you track your progress and make note of any changes you notice in your mental and emotional well-being as a result of practicing mindfulness. So choose a good quality journal that feels comfortable to write in, and a pen that you enjoy using.

Books

If you're interested in exploring more perspectives on mindfulness, here are a few books that are considered to be classics in the field:

1. "The Miracle of Mindfulness" by Thich Nhat Hanh: This book offers practical guid-

ance on how to live in the present moment and cultivate mindfulness in daily life.

2. "Wherever You Go, There You Are" by Jon Kabat-Zinn: This book offers an introduction to mindfulness and its potential benefits for mental health and well-being.

3. "Mindfulness in Plain English" by Bhante Henepola Gunaratana: This book offers a clear and straightforward explanation of mindfulness and its benefits, as well as practical guidance on how to cultivate mindfulness.

4. "The Mindful Way through Depression" by Mark Williams, John Teasdale, Zindel Segal, and Jon Kabat-Zinn: This book offers a mindfulness-based approach to dealing with depression, including practical exercises and techniques to help manage symptoms.

5. "The Mindful Path to Self-Compassion" by Christopher K. Germer: This book offers guidance on how to cultivate self-compassion through mindfulness, and how self-compassion can help reduce stress and improve overall well-being.

References

Alda, Marta, Marta Puebla-Guedea, Baltasar Rodero, Marcelo Demarzo, Jesus Montero-Marin, Miquel Roca, and Javier Garcia-Campayo. 'Zen Meditation, Length of Telomeres, and the Role of Experiential Avoidance and Compassion'. *Mindfulness* 7, no. 3 (1 June 2016): 651–59. https://doi.org/10.1007/s12671-016-0500-5.

Bartlett, Larissa, Angela Martin, Amanda L. Neil, Kate Memish, Petr Otahal, Michelle Kilpatrick, and Kristy Sanderson. 'A Systematic Review and Meta-Analysis of Workplace Mindfulness Training Randomized Controlled Trials'. *Journal of Occupational Health Psychology* 24, no. 1 (February 2019): 108–26. https://doi.org/10.1037/ocp0000146.

Brewer, Judson A., Patrick D. Worhunsky, Jeremy R. Gray, Yi-Yuan Tang, Jochen Weber, and Hedy Kober. 'Meditation Experience Is Associated with Differences in Default Mode Network Activity and Connectivity'. *Proceedings of the National Academy of Sciences* 108, no. 50 (13 December 2011): 20254–59. https://doi.org/10.1073/pnas.1112029108.

Carlson, Linda E., Tara L. Beattie, Janine Giese-Davis, Peter Faris, Rie Tamagawa, Laura J. Fick, Erin S. Degelman, and Michael Speca. 'Mindfulness-Based Cancer Recovery and Supportive-Expressive Therapy Maintain Telomere Length Relative to Controls in Distressed Breast Cancer Survivors'. *Cancer* 121, no. 3 (2015): 476–84. https://doi.org/10.1002/cncr.29063.

Cherkin, Daniel C., Karen J. Sherman, Benjamin H. Balderson, Andrea J. Cook, Melissa L. Anderson, Rene J. Hawkes, Kelly E. Hansen, and Judith A. Turner. 'Effect of Mindfulness-Based Stress Reduction vs Cognitive Behavioral Therapy or Usual Care on Back Pain and Functional Limitations in Adults With Chronic Low Back Pain: A Randomized Clinical Trial'. *JAMA* 315, no. 12 (22 March 2016): 1240–49. https://doi.org/10.1001/jama.2016.2323.

Chesin, Megan, Alejandro Interian, Anna Kline, Christopher Benjamin-Phillips, Miriam Latorre, and Barbara Stanley. 'Reviewing Mindfulness-Based Interventions for Suicidal Behavior'. *Archives of Suicide Research* 20, no. 4 (1 October 2016): 507–27. https://doi.org/10.1080/13811118.2016.1162244.

Davidson, Richard J., Jon Kabat-Zinn, Jessica Schumacher, Melissa Rosenkranz, Daniel Muller, Saki F. Santorelli, Ferris Urbanowski, Anne Harrington, Katherine Bonus, and John F. Sheridan. 'Alterations in Brain and Immune Function Produced by Mindfulness Meditation'. *Psychosomatic Medicine* 65, no. 4 (July 2003): 564–70. https://doi.org/10.1097/01.PSY.0000077505.67574.E3.

Ditto, Blaine, Marie Eclache, and Natalie Goldman. 'Short-Term Autonomic and Cardiovascular Effects of Mindfulness Body Scan Meditation'. *Annals of Behavioral Medicine* 32, no. 3 (December 2006): 227–34. https://doi.org/10.1207/s15324796abm3203_9.

Elliott, James C., B. Alan Wallace, and Barry Giesbrecht. 'A Week-Long Meditation Retreat Decouples Behavioral Measures of the Alerting and Executive Attention Networks'. *Frontiers in Human Neu-

roscience 8 (2014). https://doi.org/10.3389/fnhum. 2014.00069.

Farb, Norman A. S., Zindel V. Segal, Helen Mayberg, Jim Bean, Deborah McKeon, Zainab Fatima, and Adam K. Anderson. 'Attending to the Present: Mindfulness Meditation Reveals Distinct Neural Modes of Self-Reference'. *Social Cognitive and Affective Neuroscience* 2, no. 4 (December 2007): 313. https://doi.org/10.1093/scan/nsm030.

Gard, Tim, Britta K. Hölzel, and Sara W. Lazar. 'The Potential Effects of Meditation on Age-Related Cognitive Decline: A Systematic Review'. *Annals of the New York Academy of Sciences* 1307, no. 1 (2014): 89–103. https://doi.org/10.1111/nyas.12348.

Gard, Tim, Britta K. Hölzel, Alexander T. Sack, Hannes Hempel, Sara W. Lazar, Dieter Vaitl, and Ulrich Ott. 'Pain Attenuation through Mindfulness Is Associated with Decreased Cognitive Control and Increased Sensory Processing in the Brain'. *Cerebral Cortex (New York, N.Y.: 1991)* 22, no. 11 (November 2012): 2692–2702. https://doi.org/10.1093/cercor/bhr352.

Garland, Eric L., and Matthew O. Howard. 'Mindfulness-Based Treatment of Addiction: Current State of the Field and Envisioning the next Wave of Research'. *Addiction Science & Clinical Practice* 13, no. 1 (18 April 2018): 14. https://doi.org/10.1186/sl 3722-018-0115-3.

Goyal, Madhav, Sonal Singh, Erica M. S. Sibinga, Neda F. Gould, Anastasia Rowland-Seymour, Ritu Sharma, Zackary Berger, et al. 'Meditation Programs for Psychological Stress and Well-Being: A Systematic Review and Meta-Analysis'. *JAMA Internal Medicine* 174, no. 3 (1 March 2014): 357–68. https://doi.org/10.1001/jamainternmed.2013.13018.

Grant, Joshua A., and Pierre Rainville. 'Pain Sensitivity and Analgesic Effects of Mindful States in Zen Meditators: A Cross-Sectional Study'. *Psychosomatic Medicine* 71, no. 1 (January 2009): 106–14. https://doi.org/10.1097/PSY.0b013e31818f52ee.

Ha, Slagter, Davidson Rj, and Lutz A. 'Mental Training as a Tool in the Neuroscientific Study of Brain and Cognitive Plasticity'. *Frontiers in Human Neuroscience* 5 (2 October 2011). https://doi.org/10.3389/fnhum.2011.00017.

Jha, Amishi P., Anthony P. Zanesco, Ekaterina Denkova, Alexandra B. Morrison, Nicolas Ramos, Keith Chichester, John W. Gaddy, and Scott L. Rogers. 'Bolstering Cognitive Resilience via Train-the-Trainer Delivery of Mindfulness Training in Applied High-Demand Settings'. *Mindfulness* 11, no. 3 (1 March 2020): 683–97. https://doi.org/10.1007/s12671-019-01284-7.

Jo, Younge, Wery Mf, Gotink Ra, Utens Em, Michels M, Rizopoulos D, van Rossum Ef, Hunink Mg, and Roos-Hesselink Jw. 'Web-Based Mindfulness Intervention in Heart Disease: A Randomized Controlled Trial'. *PloS One* 10, no. 12 (12 July 2015). https://doi.org/10.1371/journal.pone.0143843.

Jw, Hughes, Fresco Dm, Myerscough R, van Dulmen Mh, Carlson Le, and Josephson R. 'Randomized Controlled Trial of Mindfulness-Based Stress Reduction for Prehypertension'. *Psychosomatic Medicine* 75, no. 8 (October 2013). https://doi.org/10.1097/PSY.0b013e3182a3e4e5.

Kabat-Zinn, J., L. Lipworth, and R. Burney. 'The Clinical Use of Mindfulness Meditation for the Self-Regulation of Chronic Pain'. *Journal of Behavioral Medicine* 8, no. 2 (June 1985): 163–90. https://doi.org/10.1007/BF00845519.

Kabat-Zinn, Jon. 'An Outpatient Program in Behavioral Medicine for Chronic Pain Patients Based on the Practice of Mindfulness Meditation: Theoretical Considerations and Preliminary Results'. *General Hospital Psychiatry* 4, no. 1 (1 April 1982):

33–47. https://doi.org/10.1016/0163-8343(82)900
26-3.

Kocovski, Nancy L., Jan E. Fleming, Lance L. Hawley, Moon-Ho Ringo Ho, and Martin M. Antony. 'Mindfulness and Acceptance-Based Group Therapy and Traditional Cognitive Behavioral Group Therapy for Social Anxiety Disorder: Mechanisms of Change'. *Behaviour Research and Therapy* 70 (July 2015): 11–22. https://doi.org/10.1016/j.brat.2015.0 4.005.

Kong, Dejun Tony. 'Ostracism Perception as a Multiplicative Function of Trait Self-Esteem, Mindfulness, and Facial Emotion Recognition Ability'. *Personality and Individual Differences*, Individual Differences in Mindfulness, 93 (1 April 2016): 68–73. https://doi.org/10.1016/j.paid.2015.08.046.

Kurth, Florian, Nicolas Cherbuin, and Eileen Luders. 'Promising Links between Meditation and Reduced (Brain) Aging: An Attempt to Bridge Some Gaps between the Alleged Fountain of Youth and the Youth of the Field'. *Frontiers in Psychology* 8 (2017). https://www.frontiersin.org/articles/10.33 89/fpsyg.2017.00860.

Kuyken, Willem, Fiona C. Warren, Rod S. Taylor, Ben Whalley, Catherine Crane, Guido Bondolfi,

Rachel Hayes, et al. 'Efficacy of Mindfulness-Based Cognitive Therapy in Prevention of Depressive Relapse: An Individual Patient Data Meta-Analysis From Randomized Trials'. *JAMA Psychiatry* 73, no. 6 (1 June 2016): 565–74. https://doi.org/10.1001/ja mapsychiatry.2016.0076.

Lao, So-An, David Kissane, and Graham Meadows. 'Cognitive Effects of MBSR/MBCT: A Systematic Review of Neuropsychological Outcomes'. *Consciousness and Cognition* 45 (1 October 2016): 109–23. https://doi.org/10.1016/j.concog.2016.08. 017.

Le Nguyen, Khoa D., Jue Lin, Sara B. Algoe, Mary M. Brantley, Sumi L. Kim, Jeffrey Brantley, Sharon Salzberg, and Barbara L. Fredrickson. 'Loving-Kindness Meditation Slows Biological Aging in Novices: Evidence from a 12-Week Randomized Controlled Trial'. *Psychoneuroendocrinology* 108 (1 October 2019): 20–27. https://doi.org/10.1016/j. psyneuen.2019.05.020.

Lebuda, Izabela, Darya L. Zabelina, and Maciej Karwowski. 'Mind Full of Ideas: A Meta-Analysis of the Mindfulness–Creativity Link'. *Personality and Individual Differences* 93 (2016): 22–26. https://do i.org/10.1016/j.paid.2015.09.040.

Liu, Shengmin, Huanhuan Xin, Li Shen, Jianjia He, and Jingfang Liu. 'The Influence of Individual and Team Mindfulness on Work Engagement'. *Frontiers in Psychology* 10 (2020). https://www.frontiersin.org/articles/10.3389/fpsyg.2019.02928.

Luders, Eileen, Nicolas Cherbuin, and Florian Kurth. 'Forever Young(Er): Potential Age-Defying Effects of Long-Term Meditation on Gray Matter Atrophy'. *Frontiers in Psychology* 5 (2015). https://www.frontiersin.org/articles/10.3389/fpsyg.2014.01551.

Lueke, Adam, and Bryan Gibson. 'Mindfulness Meditation Reduces Implicit Age and Race Bias: The Role of Reduced Automaticity of Responding'. *Social Psychological and Personality Science* 6, no. 3 (1 April 2015): 284–91. https://doi.org/10.1177/1948550614559651.

Malinowski, Peter, Adam W. Moore, Bethan R. Mead, and Thomas Gruber. 'Mindful Aging: The Effects of Regular Brief Mindfulness Practice on Electrophysiological Markers of Cognitive and Affective Processing in Older Adults'. *Mindfulness* 8, no. 1 (1 February 2017): 78–94. https://doi.org/10.1007/s12671-015-0482-8.

NCCIH. 'Meditation and Mindfulness: What You Need To Know'. Accessed 10 December 2022. https://www.nccih.nih.gov/health/meditation-and-mindfulness-what-you-need-to-know.

Morone, Natalia E., Carol M. Greco, Charity G. Moore, Bruce L. Rollman, Bridget Lane, Lisa A. Morrow, Nancy W. Glynn, and Debra K. Weiner. 'A Mind-Body Program for Older Adults With Chronic Low Back Pain: A Randomized Clinical Trial'. *JAMA Internal Medicine* 176, no. 3 (March 2016): 329–37. https://doi.org/10.1001/jamainternmed.2015.8033.

Ong, Jason C., Rachel Manber, Zindel Segal, Yinglin Xia, Shauna Shapiro, and James K. Wyatt. 'A Randomized Controlled Trial of Mindfulness Meditation for Chronic Insomnia'. *Sleep* 37, no. 9 (1 September 2014): 1553–63. https://doi.org/10.5665/sleep.4010.

PhD, B. Grace Bullock. 'How Your Breath Controls Your Mood and Attention'. *Mindful* (blog), 5 September 2019. https://www.mindful.org/how-your-breath-controls-your-mood-and-attention/.

Prakash, Ruchika Shaurya, Stephanie Fountain-Zaragoza, Arthur F. Kramer, Shaadee Samimy, and John Wegman. 'Mindfulness and Attention: Current State-of-Affairs and Future Considerations'. *Journal of Cognitive Enhancement* 4, no. 3 (1 September 2020): 340–67. https://doi.org/10.1007/s41465-019-00144-5.

Priddy, Sarah E, Matthew O Howard, Adam W Hanley, Michael R Riquino, Katarina Friberg-Felsted, and Eric L Garland. 'Mindfulness Meditation in the Treatment of Substance Use Disorders and Preventing Future Relapse: Neurocognitive Mechanisms and Clinical Implications'. *Substance Abuse and Rehabilitation* 9 (16 November 2018): 103–14. https://doi.org/10.2147/SAR.S145201.

Zeidan, Fadel, Katherine T. Martucci, Robert A. Kraft, Nakia S. Gordon, John G. McHaffie, and Robert C. Coghill. 'Brain Mechanisms Supporting the Modulation of Pain by Mindfulness Meditation'. *The Journal of Neuroscience* 31, no. 14 (6 April 2011): 5540–48. https://doi.org/10.1523/JNEUROSCI.5791-10.2011.

Zeidan, Fadel, Tim Salomons, Suzan R. Farris, Nichole M. Emerson, Adrienne Adler-Neal, Youngkyoo Jung, and Robert C. Coghill. 'Neural Mechanisms Supporting the Relationship between Dispositional Mindfulness and Pain'. *Pain* 159, no. 12

(December 2018): 2477–85. https://doi.org/10.1097/j.pain.0000000000001344.